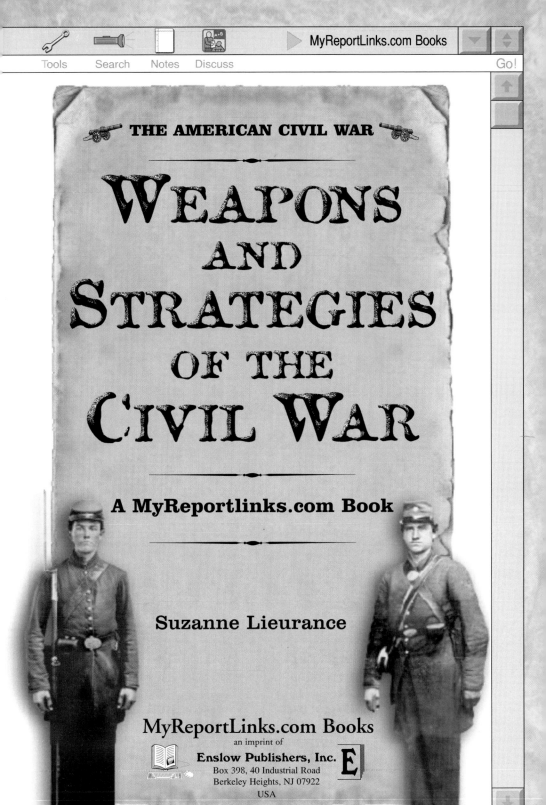

THE AMERICAN CIVIL WAR

WEAPONS AND STRATEGIES OF THE CIVIL WAR

A MyReportlinks.com Book

Suzanne Lieurance

MyReportLinks.com Books
an imprint of
Enslow Publishers, Inc.
Box 398, 40 Industrial Road
Berkeley Heights, NJ 07922
USA

MyReportLinks.com Books, an imprint of Enslow Publishers, Inc. MyReportLinks®
is a registered trademark of Enslow Publishers, Inc.

Library of Congress Cataloging-in-Publication Data

Lieurance, Suzanne.
  Weapons and strategies of the Civil War / Suzanne Lieurance.
     p. cm. — (The American Civil War)
Summary: Describes weapons used by Union and Confederate troops on land
and sea during the Civil War, as well as some of the strategies employed
by their leaders. Includes Internet links to Web sites related to the Civil War.
Includes bibliographical references and index.
  ISBN 0-7660-5185-4
  1. United States—History—Civil War, 1861–1865—Equipment and supplies—
Juvenile literature. 2. United States—Armed Forces—Weapons systems—History—19th
century—Juvenile literature. 3. Confederate States of America—Armed Forces—
Weapons systems—Juvenile literature. 4. Military weapons—United States—History—19th
century—Juvenile literature. 5. United States—History—Civil War, 1861–1865—
Campaigns—Juvenile literature. 6. Strategy—History—19th century—Juvenile literature.
[1. United States—History—Civil War, 1861–1865—Equipment and supplies.
2. United States—Armed Forces—Weapons systems—History—19th century.
3. Confederate States of America. Armed Forces—Weapons systems—History—19th century.
4. Military weapons—History—19th century. 5. United States—History—Civil War, 1861–1865
—Campaigns.] I. Title. II. American Civil War (Berkeley Heights, N.J.)
  E491.L73 2003
  973.7'3—dc22

                              2003013305

Printed in the United States of America

10 9 8 7 6 5 4 3 2 1

To Our Readers:

Through the purchase of this book, you and your library gain access to the Report Links that specifically back up this book.

The Publisher will provide access to the Report Links that back up this book and will keep these Report Links up to date on **www.myreportlinks.com** for three years from the book's first publication date.

We have done our best to make sure all Internet addresses in this book were active and appropriate when we went to press. However, the author and the Publisher have no control over, and assume no liability for, the material available on those Internet sites or on other Web sites they may link to.

The usage of the MyReportLinks.com Books Web site is subject to the terms and conditions stated on the Usage Policy Statement on **www.myreportlinks.com**.

A password may be required to access the Report Links that back up this book. The password is found on the bottom of page 4 of this book.

Any comments or suggestions can be sent by e-mail to comments@myreportlinks.com or to the address on the back cover.

Photo Credits: © Hemera Technologies, Inc., 1997–2001, p. 9; Courtesy of the National Museum of the U.S. Army, Army Art Collection, p. 17; Defense Visual Information Center/National Archives and Records Administration, pp. 14, 29, 33; Enslow Publishers, Inc., pp. 31, 38; *Illustrated Catalogue of Arms and Military Goods: Containing Regulations for the Uniform of the Army, Navy, Marine and Revenue Corps of the United States,* p. 129, reprinted by Dover Publications, Inc., p. 9; Library of Congress, pp. 1, 3, 12, 19, 39, 41, 43, 45; McClung Museum, p. 20; MyReportLinks.com Books, pp. 4, back cover; National Park Service, p. 21; Smithsonian Institution, p. 23; U.S. Naval Historical Center, pp. 24, 26.

Cover Photo: Flag, © Hemera Technologies, Inc., 1997–2001; all other images, Library of Congress.

Cover Description: Union volunteer with rifle and bayonet; Battery of sea-coast mortars during the siege of Yorktown; Union soldiers during the Peninsular Campaign, May–August, 1862.

Contents

Report Links 4

Weapons Facts 9

1   The War Begins 10

2   A Short History of American Weapons . . . 16

3   The North's Plan to Win the War 27

4   The South's Plan to Win the War 33

5   Outcome and Aftermath of the War 41

Chapter Notes 46

Further Reading 47

Index 48

MyReportLinks.com Books
Great Books, Great Links, Great for Research!

The Report Links listed on the following four pages can save you hours of research time by **instantly** bringing you to the best Web sites relating to your report topic.

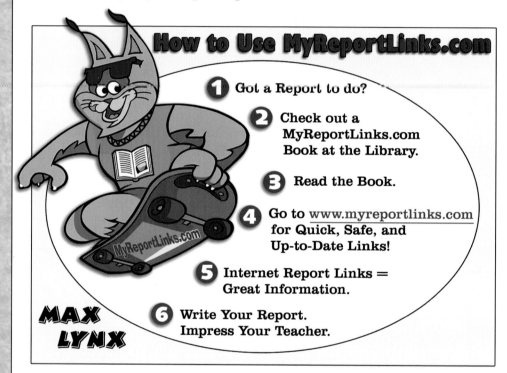

How to Use MyReportLinks.com

1 Got a Report to do?

2 Check out a MyReportLinks.com Book at the Library.

3 Read the Book.

4 Go to www.myreportlinks.com for Quick, Safe, and Up-to-Date Links!

5 Internet Report Links = Great Information.

6 Write Your Report. Impress Your Teacher.

MAX LYNX

The pre-evaluated Web sites are your links to source documents, photographs, illustrations, and maps. They also provide links to dozens—even hundreds—of Web sites about your report subject.

MyReportLinks.com Books and the MyReportLinks.com Web site save you time and make report writing easier than ever!

Please see "To Our Readers" on the copyright page for important information about this book, the MyReportLinks.com Web site, and the Report Links that back up this book. Please enter **WWS3025** if asked for a password.

Report Links

The Internet sites described below can be accessed at
http://www.myreportlinks.com

▶Weapons
*EDITOR'S CHOICE

On the Smithsonian Institution's Civil War site, you can view their collection of weapons used during the Civil War.

▶The Civil War Soldier
*EDITOR'S CHOICE

At this National Park Service Web site you will learn what it was like to be a soldier in 1863, during the Civil War. You will also learn about the weapons used in the war.

▶The Civil War
*EDITOR'S CHOICE

PBS's *Civil War* Web site provides an in-depth look at the Civil War, where you will find images, stories, facts about the war, maps, and much more.

▶The Mariners' Museum: *Monitor*
*EDITOR'S CHOICE

At the Mariners' Museum Web site you can explore naval strategies in the Civil War and learn about the ironclads, the USS *Monitor* and the CSS *Virginia*, more commonly known by its earlier name, the *Merrimac*.

▶Artillery at Antietam
*EDITOR'S CHOICE

From the National Park Service Web site you will learn about weapons used at the Battle of Antietam, including smoothbore and rifled cannon and three-inch ordnance rifles.

▶Jump Back In Time: Civil War (1860–1865)
*EDITOR'S CHOICE

America's Story from America's Library, a Library of Congress Web site, features a variety of articles about the Civil War.

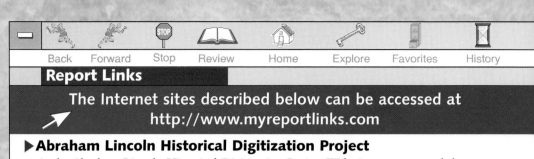
Report Links

The Internet sites described below can be accessed at http://www.myreportlinks.com

▶**Abraham Lincoln Historical Digitization Project**

At the Abraham Lincoln Historical Digitization Project Web site, you can read the writings of Abraham Lincoln.

▶**Action between USS *Monitor* and CSS *Virginia*, 9 March 1862**

The CSS *Virginia*, originally the USS *Merrimac*, and the USS *Monitor* were the first ships with iron armor. Their historic battle in 1862, which revolutionized naval warfare, is examined in this site from the United States Naval Historical Center.

▶**The Anaconda Plan**

Read about General Winfield Scott's Anaconda Plan, which he believed would help defeat the South quickly and with as little fighting as possible.

▶**Battle of Nashville:**
Union Troops Broke Through the Confederate Line

America's Story from America's Library, a Library of Congress Web site, tells the story of the Battle of Nashville, waged on December 16, 1864, in which General George H. Thomas's troops crushed the Confederate forces.

▶**Civil War: Soldier & Sailor System**

The Civil War: Soldier & Sailor System Web site provides extensive information about soldiers, sailors, cemeteries, battles, prisoners, national parks, regiments, and medals of honor.

▶**Civil War and Reconstruction**

The Civil War and Reconstruction Web site offers information about the war, its generals, weapons, and battle descriptions.

▶**The Civil War and Reconstruction: 1861–1877**

The Civil War and Reconstruction: 1861–1877 Web site chronicles the history of the Civil War.

▶**Civil War @ Smithsonian**

At the Smithsonian Web site you can explore the Civil War through images, time lines, and descriptions of events. You will also find a section devoted to the weapons of war.

Report Links

The Internet sites described below can be accessed at http://www.myreportlinks.com

▶**The Civil War in Knoxville**

The McClung Museum Web site provides information about Civil War battles in and around Knoxville, Tennessee. Here you can view artifacts and learn about weapons used in the Civil War.

▶**The Civil War in New Mexico**

The Civil War in New Mexico Web site offers a photo archive of the Civil War as it was fought in New Mexico, including weapons used in battle. You will also find maps and documents of the war.

▶**Crisis at Fort Sumter**

The first shots of the Civil War were fired on Union troops at Fort Sumter, outside Charleston, South Carolina. This Web site examines the events that led up to that battle, including background information about the crisis, Lincoln's election, and the decision to go to war.

▶**Interactive Time Machine 1855**

At the Interactive Time Machine Web site you will find a description and the schematics of the rifled musket used in the Civil War.

▶**Lincoln's Secret Weapon**

This PBS site examines what was called "Lincoln's Secret Weapon": the ironclad warship the USS *Monitor*, which revolutionized naval warfare. Here you can learn about the ship and take a virtual tour of it.

▶**The Papers of Jefferson Davis**

This site holds an archive of the writings of Jefferson Davis, the president of the Confederate States of America.

▶**Robert Edward Lee**

This brief biography of Robert E. Lee includes links to articles about Lee's ancestry, his views on slavery, and his famous horse, Traveller.

▶**Selected Civil War Photographs**

At this Library of Congress Web site you can explore images from the Civil War. You will also find a time line of events from 1861 through 1865.

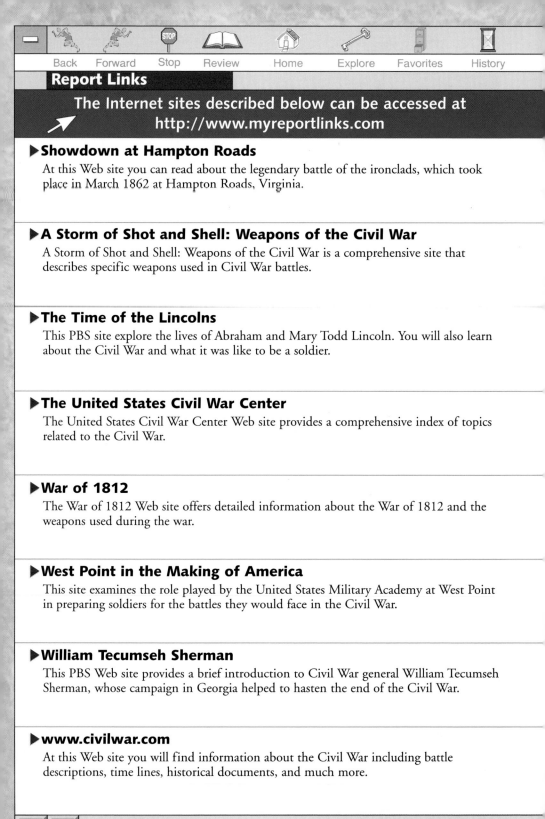

The Internet sites described below can be accessed at http://www.myreportlinks.com

▶**Showdown at Hampton Roads**

At this Web site you can read about the legendary battle of the ironclads, which took place in March 1862 at Hampton Roads, Virginia.

▶**A Storm of Shot and Shell: Weapons of the Civil War**

A Storm of Shot and Shell: Weapons of the Civil War is a comprehensive site that describes specific weapons used in Civil War battles.

▶**The Time of the Lincolns**

This PBS site explore the lives of Abraham and Mary Todd Lincoln. You will also learn about the Civil War and what it was like to be a soldier.

▶**The United States Civil War Center**

The United States Civil War Center Web site provides a comprehensive index of topics related to the Civil War.

▶**War of 1812**

The War of 1812 Web site offers detailed information about the War of 1812 and the weapons used during the war.

▶**West Point in the Making of America**

This site examines the role played by the United States Military Academy at West Point in preparing soldiers for the battles they would face in the Civil War.

▶**William Tecumseh Sherman**

This PBS Web site provides a brief introduction to Civil War general William Tecumseh Sherman, whose campaign in Georgia helped to hasten the end of the Civil War.

▶**www.civilwar.com**

At this Web site you will find information about the Civil War including battle descriptions, time lines, historical documents, and much more.

Weapons Facts

Famous—and Infamous—Weapons of the War

Bowie Knives—These edged weapons, named for Jim Bowie, hero at the Alamo, were carried by many Confederate soldiers, although hand-to-hand combat with them was rare. They were often used for opening cans.

The Dictator—This thirteen-inch seacoast mortar was used during the siege of Petersburg. The Dictator weighed over 17,000 pounds, and the shell it fired weighed more than 200 pounds. It was transported by a railroad car that was strengthened by extra beams and iron rods.

Parrott Rifles—These cast-iron cannon, named for their inventor, featured a strap of wrought iron wrapped around the breech. Unfortunately, they tended to crack upon firing, sometimes wounding or killing the artillerymen.

Ager's Coffee Mill Guns—These multi-cylinder rapid-fire weapons designed by Wilson Ager were known as the first machine guns, but they were not widely used in the war and they were not automatic—soldiers fired them by turning a hand crank. Their rapid volleys of ammunition did do damage where they were used.

Land Mines—These antipersonnel weapons were first used by the Confederate army during the Peninsula campaign. They slowed down the Union advance, but their use was condemned by many in both the North and the South.

Enfield Rifle—The Enfield rifled musket (below) was the second most widely used weapon of the Civil War. Made in England, approximately 900,000 Enfield rifles were imported during the course of the war. A single-shot muzzle-loading musket, it fired the famous .58-caliber Minié balls, often called "Minnie balls."

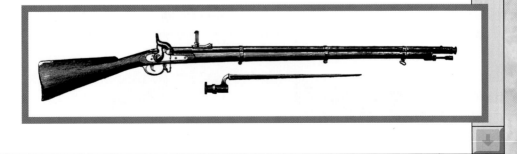

The War Begins

At 4:30 A.M. on April 12, 1861, the first shots of the Civil War were fired on Fort Sumter in Charleston Harbor, in South Carolina. After thirty-four hours of fighting, the Union troops stationed at the fort surrendered to Confederate forces. No one was killed during this first battle of the war, but over the next four years, more than 620,000 Americans would lose their lives in the struggle that divided the nation.

▶ The Road to War

By the middle of the nineteenth century, new territory added to the United States increased the divisional conflicts over states' rights, the expansion of slavery, and the power of the federal government.

Basic differences in the ways that Northerners and Southerners lived and earned their living also set the stage for the coming war. Northern states had larger cities, more people, and had become manufacturing centers. The economy of the North was not as dependent upon agriculture as the South's economy was.

The South's economy depended largely on the hot, hard work of tobacco and cotton farming. The population in the South according to the 1860 census was only 29 percent of the total population of the United States. Plantation owners felt they would not be able to find enough workers to grow and harvest their tobacco or cotton crops if they could not use slaves. Only 25 percent of Southerners owned slaves at the time, and most of those owned fewer than ten slaves. But even the majority of Southerners, who did not own slaves, would come to support and fight for the South.

By 1860, the United States had become the world's leader in the production of cotton, and that production came about as the result of 4 million African-American slaves toiling on plantations. The South was not the only beneficiary of slave labor: Textile mills in the North flourished because of the amount of cotton produced in the South.

▷ The Birth of the Confederate States of America

Eighteen sixty was also a presidential election year. The Republicans nominated Abraham Lincoln of Illinois for president. Lincoln, born in Kentucky, was not an abolitionist, but he hoped to stop the spread of slavery west as more western territories became states. Lincoln was opposed by three other candidates, most notably Stephen A. Douglas, who had defeated him for the senatorial seat in Illinois two years earlier. When Lincoln won the presidential election, the Southern states feared that he would go further and try to abolish slavery everywhere.

South Carolina voted on December 20, 1860, to secede, or leave, the Union. Within months, six Southern states—Mississippi, Florida, Alabama, Georgia, Louisiana, and Texas—followed. In February 1861, they formed their own government, the government of the Confederate States of America. They elected Jefferson Davis as president. Davis, who like Lincoln was born in Kentucky, had served as a U.S. representative and senator from Mississippi as well as secretary of war in Franklin Pierce's administration. When Davis was elected president

On February 18, 1861, Jefferson Davis was inaugurated the provisional, or temporary, president of the Confederate States of America, in Montgomery, Alabama, which was then the capital of the Confederacy.

of the Confederacy, his national reputation was more established than that of Abraham Lincoln's. But as a son of the South, Davis put his homeland above the Union when the Southern states seceded.

▷ To Preserve the Union

President Lincoln refused to accept the government of the Confederacy as valid. The Confederacy, meanwhile, considered all federal lands, including forts, that were in seceded states to be their property. When Lincoln was asked to surrender all federal forts and arsenals on what was then Confederate land, he refused and considered any attempt to take them over an act of war. On March 4, 1861, the day he took office, Lincoln gave a speech warning that he would do everything he could to "hold, occupy, and possess" federal property that happened to be on Confederate land.[1]

Since Lincoln refused to remove federal forts within the Confederacy, the new Confederacy began taking over these posts inside the South. At first, this was not difficult since most federal troops surrendered peacefully to avoid conflict.

The Battle Begins

In April 1861, Fort Sumter was an unfinished fort, located on a tiny island about three miles from the South Carolina shore. It was designed to protect the city of Charleston from enemy forces trying to enter the harbor. For that reason, all of its 140 guns faced out to sea, and their shells could not reach the shore. Major Robert Anderson refused to surrender his troops to the Confederacy, so Confederate troops cut off the fort's supply of fresh vegetables and meat. Anderson kept waiting for help from President Lincoln. He felt sure the president would make certain that food and other provisions were delivered to the fort. Finally, on April 8, Anderson received word that the president was sending ships with supplies for Anderson and his men. Two days earlier, Lincoln had sent a letter to the governor of South Carolina, assuring him that the ships would only be unloading food and other supplies, not soldiers or weapons.

For Confederate leaders, however, this action served as the breaking point. They blocked the supplies to Anderson and his men. On April 11, Confederate general Pierre G. T. Beauregard sent a message to Anderson, demanding that Union troops leave the fort.

Although Major Anderson and his men were tired and hungry, Anderson would not surrender. "I shall await the first shot, and if you do not batter us to pieces, we shall be starved out in a few days," he replied to General Beauregard.[2]

Virginian Edmund Ruffin, who was given the honor of firing the first shot at Fort Sumter, chose to end his own life in July 1865 rather than live in a country where "Yankee rule" prevailed.

Soon, Beauregard ordered his troops to fire on Fort Sumter. He offered his aide, Roger Pryor, the honor of firing the first shot. Pryor turned down the offer, but Edmund Ruffin, a sixty-seven-year-old Virginian, gladly agreed to do the job. This was merely a symbolic first shot on the fort, however. Artillery fire had already begun from other locations. Still, Ruffin is credited by many to have fired the first shot of the war.

▷ A Short Bombardment

Anderson had forty-eight of the fort's guns turned around to face the shore. Confederate forces fired on the fort, then Union forces fired back. Both sides fired back and forth like this for several days, and more than four thousand shells fell onto Fort Sumter. Surprisingly, not one person was killed during this time, although one soldier died the day following the battle, during the surrender ceremony, when a cannon backfired.

The attack on Fort Sumter was clearly an act of war. President Lincoln asked for seventy-five thousand volunteers to invade the South. Soon after, Virginia, Tennessee, Arkansas, and North Carolina, who had earlier rejected secession, joined the Confederacy. The Civil War had begun.

The Beginning of Modern Warfare

The Civil War has been called "the first of the modern wars" because it marked the beginning of modern warfare.[3] Before this war, wars were fought in a limited way. Each side needed to capture the capital or main city of the opposite side in order to win the war. The American Civil War would be different. This time, there was an unlimited goal. There was no one city or capital to be captured that would determine who would win the war, even though each side tried to capture the other's capital (Richmond for the Confederacy and Washington, D.C., for the Union). Instead, the North was fighting to preserve the Union, while the South was fighting for independence. Both sides believed that the war would last only a few months. No one on either side seemed to think it would continue for four long years.

The weapons that came to be used in the war were also more advanced than any others before, and the dawn of the ironclad ships marked a turning point in naval warfare.

A Short History of American Weapons

The Civil War was not the first war fought on American soil. Many of the same kinds of weapons used in the Civil War were created or purchased years earlier, for use in other conflicts.

▶ Weapons of the American Revolution

During the American Revolution (1775–83), when the American colonies were fighting for independence from Great Britain, American soldiers used a variety of weapons. These included muskets, rifles, pistols, cannon, and swords and other edged weapons.

▶ Muskets and Rifles

The flintlock musket with its attached bayonet was one of the main weapons of the American Revolution and was used by both American and British soldiers. This musket is known as a smoothbore, because there are no grooves or ridges on the gun's bore, which is the inner part of the barrel. A smoothbore musket could fire only one shot at a time (single-shot) and was a muzzle-loading weapon. That is, it was loaded from the muzzle, or front of the barrel. It took the average American soldier twenty seconds to load and fire a musket. To load a musket, a soldier took out a cartridge of powder from his cartridge box. The cartridge was a small paper tube that held gunpowder. The soldier then bit off the end of the cartridge and poured a small amount of gunpowder into the pan of the lock, the space where the gunpowder waits to receive sparks that ignite it. He closed the pan, dropped the cartridge (powder first) and a lead ball, the bullet, into the barrel, and rammed them down the barrel with a ramrod that was part of the gun. Then he cocked the lock of the musket so that it was ready to fire. There were no sights, or devices to aid in aiming, on the musket, so the soldier simply looked down the barrel at the intended target.

These smoothbore muskets were not at all accurate at fifty yards or more. Soldiers had to stand close together and fire their weapons all at once, which was known as firing volleys, so at least a few of the enemy would be hit. Soldiers stood shoulder to shoulder in long lines across the battlefield. Several rows of these lines allowed the front line of soldiers to fire upon the enemy while the line behind

▲ Warfare with muskets and bayonets is captured in this painting of the Battle of Bunker Hill, the first major battle of the American Revolution.

them reloaded. After the first line had fired, the next line moved up and fired, while the line behind it reloaded.

Rifles were also used in the American Revolution. They were more accurate than muskets because of the grooves in their barrels, but they were also slower to load. It took at least thirty seconds to reload a rifle. Rifles did not have bayonets, which put the soldier in great danger if the enemy charged with bayonets. A soldier wielding a rifle could be struck by an enemy's bayonet before he had a chance to reload.

The Big Guns—Cannon

Cannon were the largest and slowest weapons of the American Revolution. Muzzle-loading cannon were smoothbores. Cannon fired either a solid ball, small shot, or shells. Shells were hollow iron balls filled with black powder and fitted with a fuse. Shells exploded above the heads of advancing enemy troops. The explosions would send fragments of the shells called shrapnel into those troops.

Cannon were used mainly on ships because of their size and weight, but some were mounted on wooden frames with big wheels and used on the battlefield. It took about two minutes to clean and reload a cannon. When loaded with shot and fired at close range, a cannon could kill several of the enemy at once.

The War of 1812 and the Mexican-American War

In the War of 1812 (1812–15), the United States once again fought against the British. Many of the weapons used in this war were the same kinds of weapons used during the American Revolution. The Springfield .69 caliber musket was the standard issue of the American infantry

In 1847, Ulysses S. Grant took part in the capture of Mexico City during the Mexican-American War. Grant would go on to become the commander-in-chief of the U.S. Army during the latter part of the Civil War.

(foot soldiers) during the war. This musket was first made at the government armory in Springfield, Illinois, in 1809. During the War of 1812, private businesses began to produce this weapon. By 1814, about thirty thousand Springfield muskets were being made per year in the United States.

During the Mexican-American War, the United States Army switched from flintlock to percussion weapons. Flintlock rifles used flints in the gun's hammer to cause the spark that ignited the gunpowder and brought about the gun's charge. Percussion rifles were those in which a cap was struck to ignite the charge.

The Civil War

At the beginning of the Civil War, soldiers used many of the same weapons that had been used during the three previous wars, and experienced the same kinds of problems with those weapons. Elisha Hunt Rhodes, a Union soldier, wrote the following in his diary on July 21, 1861, during the first Battle of Bull Run. "I remember that my smoothbore gun became so foul that I was obliged to strike the ramrod against a fence to force the cartridge home, and soon exchanged it for another."[1]

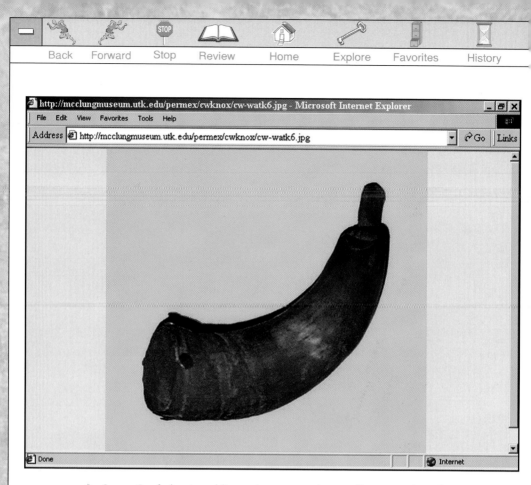

▲ *Some Confederate soldiers who were not as well equipped as their Union counterparts carried their gunpowder in horns they made themselves from cow's horns.*

The North, with more factories and more people, was able to produce many of its own weapons during the war, but the South was not. The Confederacy hoped to purchase weapons from Europe, but, for the most part, they were unable to purchase as many as they needed. As a result, some Confederate troops got their weapons by taking Northern weapons left on the battlefield. But early in the war, most Confederate troops did not want for weapons, either, as many already owned rifles and were proficient in using them.

Weapons used during the Civil War fell into these three categories: small arms (rifles and handguns); artillery (cannon, mortars, and howitzers); and edged weapons (swords and sabers).

Small Arms: Rifles and Handguns

Any weapon smaller than a cannon and carried by a soldier was known as a small arm. Small arms were identified by their caliber (the size of the shell or bullet they fired or the bore of the gun), the way they were loaded, and the maker. During the Civil War, small arms included muskets, long-barreled rifles, short-barreled rifles called carbines, and handguns (pistols and revolvers). Rifles, unlike

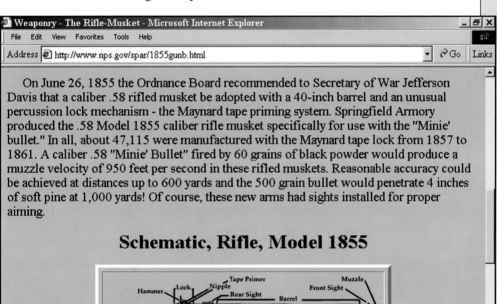

Weaponry - The Rifle-Musket - Microsoft Internet Explorer

File   Edit   View   Favorites   Tools   Help

Address http://www.nps.gov/spar/1855gunb.html   Go   Links

On June 26, 1855 the Ordnance Board recommended to Secretary of War Jefferson Davis that a caliber .58 rifled musket be adopted with a 40-inch barrel and an unusual percussion lock mechanism - the Maynard tape priming system. Springfield Armory produced the .58 Model 1855 caliber rifle musket specifically for use with the "Minie' bullet." In all, about 47,115 were manufactured with the Maynard tape lock from 1857 to 1861. A caliber .58 "Minie' Bullet" fired by 60 grains of black powder would produce a muzzle velocity of 950 feet per second in these rifled muskets. Reasonable accuracy could be achieved at distances up to 600 yards and the 500 grain bullet would penetrate 4 inches of soft pine at 1,000 yards! Of course, these new arms had sights installed for proper aiming.

Schematic, Rifle, Model 1855

Schematic drawing by John S.A. Kwiatkowski

The .58 caliber rifled musket produced by the Springfield Armory, in Massachusetts, was widely used during the Civil War.

smoothbore muskets, had spiral grooves cut into the inner surface of the barrel. These grooves made the bullet spin, which made it travel in a straighter line, making the aim more accurate. During the Civil War, the .58 caliber Springfield musket was the rifled musket widely used by both Union and Confederate troops. The .69 caliber Harpers Ferry smoothbore musket was a popular gun used by both sides, too. Both of these weapons were muzzle-loading small arms—they were loaded from the muzzle, or front of the barrel. (Weapons loaded from the back of the barrel are known as breech-loading weapons). The bullets used in the .58 caliber weapons were called minié balls, small hollow-based bullets that were quicker and easier to load than earlier bullets had been. They inflicted terrible injury.

Before the Civil War, the smoothbore muskets used in combat were so inaccurate that soldiers had to group tightly together and run directly into their enemies. The rifled muskets introduced during the Civil War were much more accurate than earlier rifles had been, so it was necessary for soldiers to change the tactics they used in battle. The rifled musket could kill at a distance of over a half-mile and was much more accurate than any earlier small arms, so direct, frontal attacks on the enemy were more deadly than ever before.

▶ Artillery

Artillery includes all firearms larger than small arms. Cannon, mortars, and howitzers were types of artillery used in the Civil War. Made of steel, iron, and bronze, artillery had different trajectories, or paths of the objects they fired. Cannon had a flat trajectory while mortars had a high arching trajectory. Howitzers had a trajectory that was between that of cannon and mortars. All cannon used during the

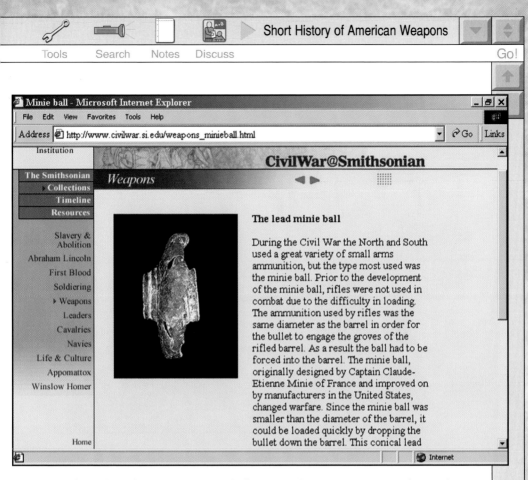

Bullets known as Minié balls were the most common form of ammunition used in small arms during the Civil War. They were named for their French designer, Captain Claude-Etienne Minié.

Civil War were either smoothbore or rifled. They were also identified by the weight of the object they fired, so they were known as twelve pounders, twenty-four pounders, thirty-two pounders, and so on. They were also identified by the caliber or diameter of the barrel or bore (three inch, eight inch, ten inch), the method of loading (breech or muzzle), and sometimes the name of the inventor or factory where they were made (Dahlgren, Napoleon, Rodman, Parrott, Whitworth). Civil War artillery was also classified according to how and where it was used in battle.

File Edit View Favorites Tools Help

Address http://www.history.navy.mil/photos/images/h00001/h00574.jpg

Go | Links

Done | Internet

The crew of the USS Monitor *is seen at rest on the Union ironclad. The gunboat's heavily armored turret, twenty feet in diameter, is behind them. The turret, powered by steam, was able to rotate and fire its eleven-inch Dalhgren shell guns, the heaviest weapons then made.*

▶ Edged Weapons

Edged weapons are just what they sound like—weapons with sharp edges. Edged weapons used during the Civil War included bayonets, sabers, swords, short swords, cutlasses, Bowie knives, pikes, and lances. Swords were mainly a symbol of an officer's rank in the Civil War. They were not as effective as rifles or muskets, and the fire coming from these arms made it difficult for soldiers to engage in hand-to-hand combat. Bayonets, as well, were not the effective weapons that they had been in earlier wars.

► Machine Guns

The machine gun was a new weapon at the time of the Civil War. In October 1861, President Lincoln bought ten of these guns, which he called "coffee-mill" guns.[2] His order was the first machine-gun order in history. However, Union troops were reluctant to try new weapons and never took full advantage of any of the various types of machine guns that developed during the war.

► Ships and Submarines

Conventional wooden battleships were used during the war and were easily damaged. Then, a new era in naval warfare began when both the Union and Confederate navies discovered they could cover ships with iron, producing what they called "ironclads." The Union launched its ironclad, the USS *Monitor*, on January 30, 1862—the same day the South launched its ironclad, the *Merrimac*. (Once a Union warship, the *Merrimac* had been captured by the Confederates, rebuilt, and renamed the CSS *Virginia*.) On March 9, 1862, these two ironclads battled each other in the waters off Hampton Roads, Virginia, from eight in the morning until noon. Finally, both ships turned away in a draw and never fought each other again. A few months later the *Merrimac* was sunk by its own crew so that it would not be captured by the Union. Both sides continued to produce ironclads, but the Union made more of theirs, which were better constructed.

► The First Sub

Submarines were first used in warfare during the Civil War. After the opening battle at Fort Sumter, President Lincoln ordered a Union blockade of Southern ports, and

△ *On the morning of April 8, 2000, the* H. L. Hunley *was raised from the ocean floor off of Charleston, South Carolina.*

Charleston was the main Southern port at the time. The Confederate sub the *H. L. Hunley* was launched as an attempt to break the blockade. On February 17, 1864, it torpedoed and sank the Union warship the USS *Housatonic,* scoring the first military victory in history by a submarine. But the *Hunley* and her nine-man crew went down, too. The submarine was discovered in the waters off Charleston in 1995 and recovered in 2000. Her crew will be given full military honors in a burial ceremony in Charleston in 2004.

Chapter 3 ▶

The North's Plan to Win the War

As the Civil War began, President Lincoln wanted to figure out a way to win the war quickly and force the Confederate states back into the Union. He met with his generals and other advisers to devise a strategy, or plan, to make this happen.

▷ "Scott's Great Snake": The Anaconda Plan

General Winfield Scott was the commanding general of the Union army at the beginning of the war. He had an idea, which the press nicknamed the Anaconda Plan, after the large South American snake that squeezes the life out of its prey. General Scott, born in Virginia, felt that most Southerners wanted to be back in the Union. His plan was to make this happen with as little fighting as possible.

The Union would focus its attack on the South's resources instead of its armies. The Anaconda Plan would create a complete naval blockade of the 3,500 miles of Southern seacoast, cutting off all contact between the Confederate states and the outside world. It was hoped that this blockade would squeeze the life out of the Confederacy as it prevented exports of Southern cotton to textile mills in Europe, which were a major source of Confederate income. It would also prevent imports of food and other goods that the Confederacy needed for everyday life and for the war. Eventually, without food and other necessities, the South would be forced to surrender and rejoin the Union.

On April 19, 1861, President Abraham Lincoln issued a proclamation calling for the blockade. In this proclamation, he said, "A competent force will be posted so as to prevent entrance and exit of vessels from the ports aforesaid."[1] Gideon Welles, secretary of the U.S. Navy, was in charge of creating and maintaining the blockade. In order for the blockade to be successful, the navy had to expand its fleet, which consisted of fewer than ninety ships in the spring of 1861. More than half of them were obsolete wooden sailing vessels. So, at the start of the war, civilian fishing boats and ferries were armed and used to help the navy enforce the blockade.

Some Southern business owners had fast ships that could make it through the Union blockade to Confederate ports and deliver much-needed supplies. These ships were called blockade-runners. At first, most blockade-runners made it through the blockade, but by 1864, the navy had many more ships in its fleet and was catching one runner out of every two. By the end of the war, the Union navy had more than six hundred ships in its fleet.

Manassas/Bull Run

On July 21, 1861, Union and Confederate troops met near a small railway center in Manassas, Virginia. General Irvin McDowell and his Union army attacked the Confederates across a small stream called Bull Run Creek. Finally, the public would have something to see. Civilians brought picnic baskets and spread blankets out on the grass, eager to watch the fighting which they thought would bring an end to the war by the afternoon. At first, the Union army had the upper hand. As Union corporal Samuel J. English wrote in a letter to his mother, "On our arrival into the open field I saw I should judge three or four thousand rebels retreating for a dense woods, firing as they retreated."[2] But, after a few hours, fresh Confederate troops arrived by railroad and launched a counterattack. They forced the Union army to retreat to Washington. The civilians raced back there, too. But, perhaps because of their defensive strategy, plus the fatigue of battle, the Confederates became confused and failed to follow and defeat the retreating Union soldiers.

▷ Controlling the Mississippi

The second step of the Anaconda Plan was to take control of the Mississippi River so that Texas, Louisiana, and Arkansas would have trouble transporting supplies and troops. The Confederates would be forced to use roads and trails, which would slow them down. They would also need many mules and horses. And, if the North gained control of the Mississippi River, Confederate troops could not join together to make

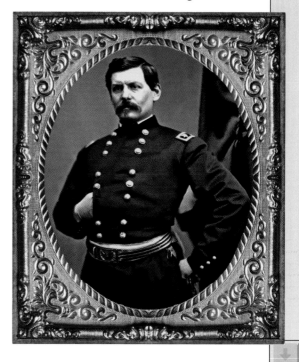

General McClellan's ▷ *failure to have his armies advance at crucial moments led President Lincoln to dismiss him.*

one large army. When Union forces under the command of General Ulysses S. Grant were victorious in capturing Vicksburg, Mississippi, a key port on the river, in July 1863, the Union was finally in control of the Mississippi River. Grant's victory, which came a day after the Southern defeat at Gettysburg, accomplished the second phase of the Anaconda Plan.

The third step in the Union's plan was to destroy the Confederate government by capturing Richmond, its capital. General George McClellan was put in charge of this task, and he worked hard to develop a strong army. He trained and drilled his men for months so that they would be ready to attack Richmond. But McClellan and his men were never able to capture the Confederate capital. It would not be seized until April 2, 1865, when General Ulysses S. Grant and his forces finally took the city.

▷ Union Strengths

At the start of the Civil War, the Union held many advantages over the Confederacy. The North had a much larger population than the South: About 20 million people lived in the Northern states while only about 9 million lived in the Southern states. The larger population meant that there were more people to fight in the Union army and more people to work for the war effort and keep the economy going.

There were many farms in the North. Northern farmers often raised enough food to feed their own families plus extra food to sell in the cities. Northern farms would continue to produce food for the Union during the war, even though many farmers left their homes to fight. Often, women and children would do the farming when the men went off to war.

The North also had many more factories than the South. Factories in Northern cities produced large numbers of goods, and, as the war started, more people were hired to work in these factories. Factory owners bought more machines so even more goods could be produced for the war. Factories in the North made everything from uniforms, underwear, boots, and shoes to wagons, shovels, and surgical instruments. They also manufactured weapons and ammunition, which gave the North a huge advantage over the South.

There were more railroads, roads, rivers, canals, and other means of transportation in the North, too, so food, goods, and soldiers could be easily transported.

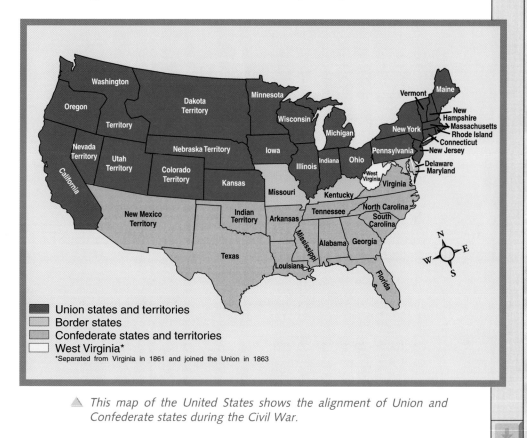

Union states and territories
Border states
Confederate states and territories
West Virginia*
*Separated from Virginia in 1861 and joined the Union in 1863

▲ This map of the United States shows the alignment of Union and Confederate states during the Civil War.

Finally, there was already an established government in the North, under the leadership of President Lincoln, and an established military. The Confederacy had the task of setting up its government while waging war, which put it at a disadvantage from the start.

Union Weaknesses

Despite its strengths, the North did have some weaknesses. For one thing, the United States Army lost some experienced generals when Robert E. Lee and others agreed to serve on the side of the Confederacy. Soldiers from the North who had worked in factories and lived in cities before the war had less experience using guns, riding horses, or living outdoors than most Confederate soldiers, although many Union soldiers who came from rural western areas, including Ulysses S. Grant, were accustomed to guns and horses. Some Union soldiers were also recent immigrants to the United States, so they did not know how to speak English, which often made communication among the troops difficult.

With the rush to produce military supplies, many of the factories in the North worked too quickly, turning out products that were not made very well. They fell apart easily or did not work correctly. There were also dishonest business owners who charged outrageously high prices for poorly made or worn-out supplies. They would buy large quantities of materials, such as leather, that they knew would be needed for manufacturing goods, such as shoes. They would hoard, or keep, these materials until the price for them went up. When the price became very high, they sold the materials and made a huge profit. Many business owners became wealthy this way, charging high prices that made life during the war even more difficult for most everyone else.

The South's Plan to Win the War

With limited resources and a newly formed—in many ways, still forming—government, the Confederacy's strategies for winning the war differed from those of the Union.

▶ A Long War on Southern Soil

The South, unlike the North, wanted to fight a long-drawn-out defensive war. The states in the Confederacy would defend their right to withdraw from the Union and protect their borders. A clear advantage for the South over the North from the onset was that Southerners would be fighting mostly on their own soil,

Although General Robert ▶ E. Lee was not made commander-in-chief of all Southern armies until late in the war, his leadership in Virginia kept the Union army at bay there for three long years.

with the purpose of becoming an independent country, and their morale was high.

The South planned to force the North to stay on the move and fight battles on poor ground. The plan was that Confederate troops would never engage the enemy in long battles and would always stay on the move. The South thought that the Union army would grow tired of the struggle and would eventually give up if the Confederates could just drag things out long enough.

A Dispersed Defensive

The South started its military strategy with a "dispersed defensive." This strategy sent many small groups of troops to the borders of the Confederacy to try to keep the Union troops from invading. Confederate troops were stationed in forts along the seacoast and on rivers. Other Southern soldiers defended the railways, mountain passes, or river crossings on or near Confederate borders.

When the South managed to force Union troops to retreat toward Washington, D.C., after the war's first major battle, the First Battle of Manassas/Bull Run on July 21, 1861, the Union's military leadership was shocked. They had not counted on the strength of the Confederate army. The South's strategy seemed to be working at this point.

Offensive-Defensive Strategy

As the war went on, modifications were made to the dispersed defensive, so the South's strategy changed to an "offensive-defensive" strategy. This meant that sometimes the South would attack the enemy in Confederate territory.

In February 1862, General Ulysses S. Grant and his Union troops were taking over forts and other sites along the Mississippi River. Camped at Pittsburg Landing, Tennessee, they planned to wait there for reinforcements. Grant believed that the Confederates would not attack since they usually preferred a defensive strategy, so he was not very concerned about the enemy's location. His forces were spread out in a large area around a meeting place called Shiloh Church. But before reinforcements arrived, the Confederates surprised Grant, and a two-day battle took place. The Confederates fought successfully the first day even though their commander, General Albert S. Johnston, was killed and they were exhausted. When Grant's reinforcements arrived on the second day, the

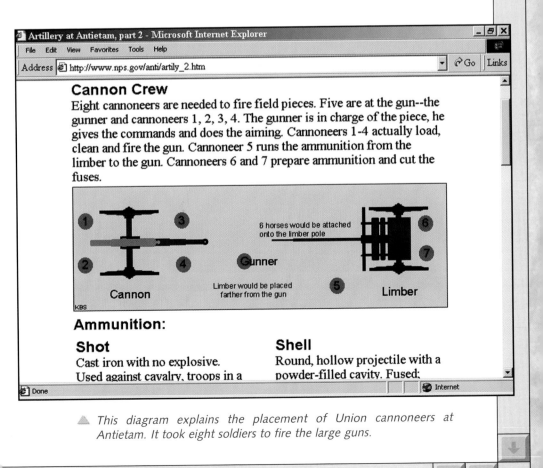

Artillery at Antietam, part 2 - Microsoft Internet Explorer

File   Edit   View   Favorites   Tools   Help

Address http://www.nps.gov/anti/artily_2.htm   Go   Links

Cannon Crew

Eight cannoneers are needed to fire field pieces. Five are at the gun--the gunner and cannoneers 1, 2, 3, 4. The gunner is in charge of the piece, he gives the commands and does the aiming. Cannoneers 1-4 actually load, clean and fire the gun. Cannoneer 5 runs the ammunition from the limber to the gun. Cannoneers 6 and 7 prepare ammunition and cut the fuses.

6 horses would be attached onto the limber pole

Gunner

Cannon   Limber would be placed farther from the gun   Limber

KBS

Ammunition:

Shot
Cast iron with no explosive.
Used against cavalry, troops in a

Shell
Round, hollow projectile with a
powder-filled cavity. Fused;

Done   Internet

This diagram explains the placement of Union cannoneers at Antietam. It took eight soldiers to fire the large guns.

battle ended in defeat for the Confederates. This time, the offensive-defensive strategy had failed.

There was another change in strategy, when, in the fall of 1862, for the first time during the war, the South made a coordinated effort to attack the North outside Confederate soil in Maryland. General Lee hoped that winning a battle there would make the English and French governments see the South as a separate country, fighting to protect its rights, and would offer much-needed supplies and money to help the Confederates fight the war.

▷ Antietam and Perryville: Confederate Strategy Fails

On September 17, a battle at Antietam Creek near Sharpsburg, Maryland, took place between McClellan's Union troops and half of the Confederate army under the command of General Robert E. Lee. The Battle of Antietam is known as the bloodiest single day in American history—more than 23,000 men were killed, wounded, or missing in action on that September day. Antietam was a costly defeat for Lee and a strategic victory for the Union because it led Abraham Lincoln to issue his first draft of the Emancipation Proclamation.

Then, on October 8, a battle took place in Perryville, Kentucky, between the Union forces of General Don Carlos Buell and Confederate forces of General Braxton Bragg in which more than 7,500 Union and Confederate troops were killed or wounded. That battle ended in a standoff, although it was considered a strategic victory for the Union because the outnumbered Confederate troops were driven from Kentucky, which remained in Union control for the rest of the war.

▷ The Emancipation Proclamation

After Antietam and Perryville, the South's hope of getting help from Europe began to fade and finally died when in January 1863, Lincoln issued the Emancipation Proclamation. It declared that "all persons held as slaves within any state or designated part of a State, the people whereof shall then be in rebellion against the United

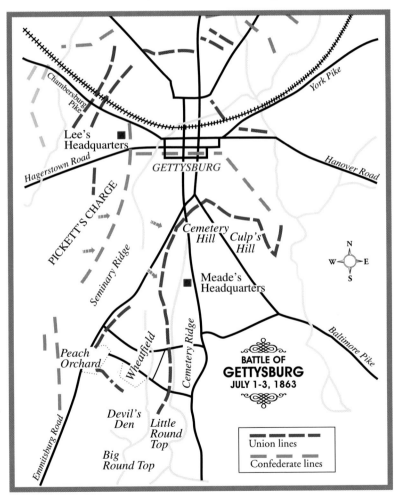

▲ The battleground of the war's pivotal battle, the Battle of Gettysburg, is shown in this map. The Confederate forces were to the north, and the Union forces were south of the town.

States, shall be then, thenceforward, and forever free. . . ."[1] Although the proclamation was limited, it changed the character of the war. Every Union soldier was now engaged in a fight against slavery. African Americans were recruited by the Union army and navy to fight for their freedom.

Defeat at Gettysburg

General Robert E. Lee tried once more to take the offensive. He took seventy-five thousand men and marched north. Along the way he hoped to resupply his troops. In Gettysburg, Pennsylvania, Confederate and Union armies accidentally crossed paths, and both sides quickly organized and reinforced their forces outside of town. The Union commander, with about 85,000 men, was General George G. Meade. The horrible battle lasted three days, with total losses of more than fifty thousand soldiers. Pickett's Charge, an ill-fated Confederate attack on the center of the Union line on the third day of the battle, was Lee's strategy. The Confederate troops were led across an open field, but most of the men were killed by artillery and rifle fire before they could reach the Union lines. The Confederate army never recovered from the heavy losses it suffered that day.

Strategy of Attrition

By 1864, the South had such a shortage of resources that its main strategy was the strategy of attrition, which involved wearing down the enemy to the point of exhaustion. Confederate troops would only fight when it was necessary to do so in order to prevent the enemy from overtaking Southern territory. Masses of Confederate troops dug defensive positions in trenches where they could defend their territory without starting new battles.

Confederate Advantages

The South's greatest advantage was that nearly all of the fighting in the war would take place on familiar soil, so Confederate soldiers would be defending their homeland, which also gave them more incentive to fight. They knew the terrain, could retreat more safely when they needed to, and were closer to food supplies, at least in the beginning.

The South's motives for fighting were also much clearer to many of its soldiers—they were not fighting to preserve a concept, "the Union," but to preserve their very way of life, which they saw as threatened by the federal government of the United States.

Finally, in Robert E. Lee, the South had perhaps the greatest commander of the war. Lee had been offered command of the Union army by President Lincoln at the outset of the war, but his loyalties to his home state, Virginia, compelled him to decline.

Known as breastworks, these fortifications were built by Confederate troops during the siege of Petersburg. Soldiers lived underneath the small mounds that are topped by chimneys.

Confederate Disadvantages

At the start of the war, the South was at a great disadvantage in its lack of manufacturing and transportation centers. In 1860, only one tenth of the goods manufactured in the United States were produced in the South. To make things worse, there were few railroads in the South for transporting the goods produced there.

While the North could produce the food, equipment, and weapons it would need for the war (and for those who would remain at home during the war), the South could not. Unlike the farms in the North that produced large quantities of food, many of the South's big plantations grew only enough food to feed their own families and their slaves. Most of the cash crops produced on these plantations were tobacco and cotton, not food. The Confederacy would have to buy some of its weapons in Europe with money earned by selling its cotton crop. But the Union navy was already blocking the South's trade with Europe, and the Confederacy had almost no navy to defend its coast. This meant that very often, the Confederacy, and civilians living in Confederate states, went without the food and supplies they desperately needed. On July 16, 1861, Mary Chesnut, a woman who kept a diary about life in the Confederacy during the war, wrote, "Already they begin to cry out for more ammunition, and already the blockade is beginning to shut it all out."[2]

Finally, with only 9 million people, the South also had less than half the population of the North, and of that 9 million, 4 million were African-American slaves. So the South had fewer men to call upon to serve as soldiers.

Outcome and Aftermath of the War

Things got even worse for the South in 1864, when President Lincoln named General Ulysses S. Grant general-in-chief of all Union armies. Grant made plans for several attacks to be made all at once on Southern forces from different positions in the Southern states—an all-fronts campaign. Grant's strength was in realizing that the North could eventually defeat the South because of the North's much larger force. In May, Grant marched toward Richmond with 119,000 Union soldiers. He wanted to take over the Confederate capital and overpower General Robert E. Lee, who had just 64,000 men.

▶ Sherman Burns Atlanta

Grant had ordered other troops to attack in Alabama and Tennessee. He also ordered General William Tecumseh Sherman and his men to march through Georgia. The plan was for Sherman to defeat General Joseph E. Johnston's army, then capture the South's last major

◀ *Under Grant's command, William Tecumseh Sherman introduced a new kind of warfare when he and his troops marched through Georgia to Savannah, leaving a path of destruction in their wake.*

railway center in Atlanta. Grant told Sherman to inflict all the damage on the South that he could, driving the Southerners beyond any means to resist.

Sherman and about 100,000 soldiers marched through Georgia, destroying everything they came across. They reached Atlanta on July 17 and by September 1, they had forced Confederate general John Bell Hood and his troops to leave the city. Sherman then told all civilians to leave the city, and he ordered his men to burn Atlanta to the ground. Sherman's troops also destroyed bridges, factories, and warehouses, cut telegraph lines, and tore up miles of railroad track. General Grant sent a letter of congratulations to Sherman, which read, "I have just received your dispatch announcing the capture of Atlanta. In honor of your great victory, I have ordered a salute to be fired. . . ."[1]

Sherman's March to the Sea

Sherman and his men continued their march to Savannah, arriving on December 10. When Sherman and his troops took over the city, it left Confederate forces in only three states—North Carolina, South Carolina, and the southern half of Virginia.

Grant's troops finally took Richmond in April and set fire to the city. Now, much of the South lay in ruins, and Lee's army was on the run. Grant and Lee exchanged messages until it was agreed that they meet to discuss terms of surrender. General Lee felt that the entire South would be destroyed if he did not surrender.

Lee Surrenders

On April 9, 1865, General Robert E. Lee surrendered to General Ulysses S. Grant at Appomattox Court House, Virginia. The terms of surrender were not harsh, and the men in Lee's army who owned their own horses were allowed to keep them. Some small battles took place for several more weeks, however, and the war was not officially declared over until May.

It had been a costly and bloody four years. The war had claimed more than 600,000 lives (about 360,000 for the North and 258,000 for the South), although most did not die in battle. Starvation, disease, and other factors led to thousands of deaths. Soldiers on both sides who had managed to survive were ready to go home. Most were not ready, however, for what they would find when they got there.

Returning Home

When Union soldiers returned to their homes, they found that the population in the North had greatly increased and industry was booming. During the four years of the war, European immigrants had flooded into the North.

As a result, many of the North's large cities were overcrowded, and thousands of people were living in poverty. Still, things in the North were far better than they were in the South.

What remained of the South must have

The ravages of war are seen in this photograph taken of Charleston, South Carolina, in April 1865. It would take years for the South to recover, both physically and emotionally.

been a terrible shock for many Confederate soldiers when they returned to their homes—if, indeed, they had homes to return to. Large parts of many Southern states were destroyed. Many homes had been deserted, looted, and burned and were now mere ashes and rubble. Banks, railroads, and factories had shut down. There were also hundreds of thousands of former slaves who had nowhere to go, no real skills, no education, and no jobs.

Lincoln Is Assassinated

On the night of April 14, 1865, just five days after Lee's surrender, President Lincoln was mortally wounded while watching a play at Ford's Theatre in Washington, D.C. An actor named John Wilkes Booth, who sympathized with the South, shot Lincoln in the back of the head and then leaped out of the box toward the stage.

President Lincoln was carried to a house across the street from the theater. Although many doctors visited him, there was nothing any of them could do. Lincoln died about nine hours later, on April 15. Booth was found on April 26 and killed in a barn. His diary was also found. In it, Booth had written about Lincoln, "Our country owed all her troubles to him, and God simply made me the instrument of His punishment."[2]

Reconstruction and Recovery

President Lincoln had been working on a plan for rebuilding the South and the nation even before Lee surrendered. Lincoln's plan was called the "Proclamation of Amnesty and Reconstruction." This plan would require 10 percent of the men who voted in a Confederate state during 1860 to swear loyalty to the United States. If they did, then that state could organize a new state government.

After President Lincoln's assassination, Vice President Andrew Johnson became president. He developed a new Proclamation of Amnesty plan. Under his plan, 50 percent of voters in a Confederate state had to swear loyalty to the United States. Former Confederate leaders and other important Southerners would need to apply for individual pardons. They also had to accept the Thirteenth Amendment, which abolished slavery. It was ratified on December 6, 1865, and went into effect on December 18.

All former Confederate states eventually returned to the Union under Johnson's plan. It took many years for the bitterness between North and South to lessen, and many decades for life to improve for African Americans in the United States.

The Northern strategies employed during the Civil War led to the eventual Union victory and the preservation of the United States, but not before the army's leadership changed hands many times. The Southern strategy— to draw the war out as long as possible—worked until there were simply not enough men to fight on the side of the Confederacy any more.

No one at the start of the ▶ *Civil War—including Abraham Lincoln—thought the conflict would last as long as it did.*

Chapter 1. The War Begins

1. Abraham Lincoln, *Speeches and Writings 1859–1865* (New York: The Library of America, 1989), p. 218.

2. A. R. Chisolm, Colonel, C.S.A., "Notes on the Surrender of Fort Sumter," n.d., <www.ehistory.com/uscw/library/books/battles/vol1/082.cfm> (March 30, 2003).

3. Trevor Dupuy, *The Evolution of Weapons and Warfare* (Indianapolis: The Bobbs-Merrill Company, Inc., 1980), p. 196.

Chapter 2. A Short History of American Weapons

1. Robert Hunt Rhodes, *All for the Union: The Civil War Diary and Letters of Elisha Hunt Rhodes* (New York: Orion Books, 1989), p. 26.

2. "Machine Guns," *The Civil War: Strange and Fascinating Facts*, n.d., <http://165.29.91.7/classes/humanities/amstud/9798/weapons/machin~1.htm> (March 28, 2003).

Chapter 3. The North's Plan to Win the War

1. Abraham Lincoln, *Speeches and Writings 1859–1865* (New York: The Library of America, 1989), p. 234.

2. Robert Hunt Rhodes, *All for the Union: The Civil War Diary and Letters of Elisha Hunt Rhodes* (New York: Orion Books, 1989), p. 33.

Chapter 4. The South's Plan to Win the War

1. Abraham Lincoln, *Speeches and Writings 1859–1865* (New York: The Library of America, 1989), p. 424.

2. C. Vann Woodward, ed., *Mary Chesnut's Civil War* (New Haven & London: Yale University Press, 1981), p. 101.

Chapter 5. Outcome and Aftermath of the War

1. Ulysses S. Grant, *Memoirs and Selected Letters, 1839–1865* (New York: The Library of America, 1990), p. 1067.

2. "Ford's Theatre and Beyond," *The Lincoln Museum*, n.d., <http://www.thelincolnmuseum.org/new/exhibits/fords_theatre/index.html> (March 31, 2003).

Further Reading

Arnold, James R. and Roberta Wiener. *On to Richmond: The Civil War in the East, 1861–1862.* Minneapolis: Lerner Publications Company, 2002.

——————. *Life Goes On: The Civil War at Home, 1861–1865.* Minneapolis: Lerner Publications Company, 2002.

Bolotin, Norman. *Civil War A to Z.* New York: Dutton, 2002.

Brewer, Paul. *American Civil War—History of Warfare.* Austin: Raintree Steck-Vaughn, 1999.

Carter, Alden R. *The Civil War: American Tragedy.* New York: Franklin Watts, 1992.

Gay, Kathlyn, and Martin Gay. *Civil War.* New York: Twenty-First Century Books, 1995.

Gienapp, William E. *Abraham Lincoln and Civil War America, a Biography.* Oxford and New York: Oxford University Press, 2002.

Hakim, Joy. *A History of US: War, Terrible War.* Oxford and New York: Oxford University Press, 2003.

Peacock, Judith. *Reconstruction: Rebuilding After the Civil War.* Minnetonka, Minn.: Capstone Press, 2003.

Wisler, G. Clifton. *When Johnny Went Marching: Young Americans Fight the Civil War.* New York: HarperCollins, 2001.

A

American Revolution, 16, 17, 18
Anaconda Plan, 27, 29, 30
Anderson, Major Robert, 13, 14
Antietam, Battle of, 35, 36
Appomattox Court House, 42

B

Battle of Bunker Hill, 17
Beauregard, General Pierre G. T.,
    13, 14
blockade-runners, 28
Booth, John Wilkes, 44
Bragg, General Braxton, 36
Buell, General Don Carlos, 36

C

coffee-mill guns, 25
Confederate States of America, 11
CSS *Virginia*, 25

D

Davis, Jefferson, 11, 12, 21
dispersed-defensive, 34
Douglas, Stephen A., 11

E

Emancipation Proclamation,
    37, 38

F

Fort Sumter, 10, 13, 14, 15, 26

G

Gettysburg, Battle of, 37, 38
Grant, Ulysses S., 19, 29, 30, 32,
    34, 35, 41, 42

H

Hood, John Bell, 42
H. L. Hunley, 26

I

ironclads, 15, 25

J

Johnson, Andrew, 45
Johnston, General Albert S., 35
Johnston, General Joseph E., 41

L

Lee, General Robert E., 32, 33, 36,
    38, 39, 41, 42, 44
Lincoln, Abraham, 11, 12, 13, 14,
    26, 27, 29, 31, 36, 37, 39, 40,
    41, 44, 45

M

Manassas/Bull Run, Battles of,
    28, 34
McClellan, General George,
    29, 36
McDowell, General Irvin,
    28, 29, 30
Meade, General George G., 38
Mexican-American War, 19
Minié balls, 21, 23
Minié, Captain Claude-Etienne, 23

O

offensive-defensive strategy, 34

P

Perryville, Battle of, 36
Pickett's Charge, 38
Proclamation of Amnesty and
    Reconstruction, 44
Pryor, Roger, 14

R

Ruffin, Edmund, 14

S

Scott, General Winfield, 27
Sherman, General William
    Tecumseh, 41, 42
submarines, 26

U

USS *Housatonic*, 26
USS *Merrimac* (CSS *Virginia*), 25
USS *Monitor*, 24, 25

W

War of 1812, 18, 19
Welles, Gideon, 28